D1132204

How to Heal Your Human

HOW TO HEAL YOUR HUMAN

A Dog's Advice for Achieving Well*being*

Eamon the Wheaten
with
Sandra Marticio

Illustrated by Churmy Fan
Edited by Kate Agathon and Greg Feldman
Cover design and interior design by Patrick Scheff
Cover photos by Greg Feldman

CONTENTS

FOREWORD

I met Sandra and Eamon in 2017 when they applied for the Jefferson County volunteer Bark Patroller program. What made them stand out from other volunteers was their unmistakable bond. Our program often helps improve the bond between volunteers and their dogs, but it was obvious they already understood the complexity of the emotional relationship between dogs and humans.

Regardless of the duration of our relationship, dogs and humans are bonded on many levels. Dogs are our workers and our companions. One can even say that how a society treats its dogs greatly reflects that culture's health and socioeconomic status. I see this bond as the foundation of our ability to help one another. Because we are connected, we have a responsibility to care for our canine companions. Sandra and Eamon explore—and live— this bond at a visceral level. This book describes specific ways to grow, bond, and heal with a canine leader.

On a personal level, I am so grateful to my own rescues, Avery and Baxter—they've rescued me so many times! Most recently, they led me through the tears and emotional trauma of my mother's cancer treatments and subsequent passing. There were some days that I am certain I would not have gotten out of bed were it not for them. I also have a newfound appreciation for my late mother's rescue dog, GiGi. While GiGi couldn't cure my mom, she provided a unique and effective type of support and comfort, thereby alleviating some suffering in my mom's final days. And that brought me comfort, too.

We all face challenges in life, whether they be emotional or physical. I hope you will allow your dog to help heal you—and this book will show you how! Listen closely to the canines, for they have wisdom to share.

Happy Tails!

Shaun Howard
Park Ranger Lead, Jefferson County Open Space
Golden, Colorado

Prologue

My name is Eamon. It's pronounced *Ee-min*, although *Ay-mon* also is correct. My peeps just call me *E*. The story of my name is a long one, but the short version is that Eamon is Gaelic for Edward. Coincidentally, I share my birthday with two other Edwards in the family—one on each side—and being an Irish breed, the name seemed like a good fit.

I'm a healer. Please don't confuse that with "heeler"—that's different! My person is Sandra but I just call her *S*. S adopted me from a breeder when I was four and she thought she was getting a pet. Much to her surprise, the day she picked me up, she was told I'd been trained to be a therapy dog. To some degree, we all have the capacity to be "therapy dogs." Please keep in mind, however, that I am not a licensed therapist or a psychiatrist. If your human is suffering from clinical depression or severe mental illness or if they believe they may harm you, themselves, or another person, please encourage them to get professional help immediately.

About three years ago I came to live with S and her husband, Patrick, who I simply refer to as *P*. I'm active on Twitter and am accustomed to character conservation, so that works well. Shortly after my arrival, a series of events happened in the lives of S and P that set in motion a cycle of deep disappointment, loss, grief, and even some health issues. There was the loss of jobs they both really loved (and for S, the loss of a subsequent job she didn't really love), broken friendships, canceled "bucket list" trips, family drama, and death. When S set out to break this negative cycle and experience greater peace and joy, I immediately saw an opportunity to help. I love to help! Plus, I have seen S as my "pet project" since I first arrived here.

As a long-time cyclist, S has always been physically fit. She came to realize that there is a distinction between physical fitness and well*being*. As someone who loves endurance events, she became accustomed to having a strong and responsive body that would do whatever she asked of it *if* she had the mental capacity to push through pain. She became very comfortable with her mind working through physical pain and with using physical pain to quiet her mind. After many years, that cycle became an unhealthy one for her. This book highlights the method we used to achieve her well*being*—a more holistic existence in which she allows herself to feel whatever arises and works through it naturally. Although she really just wanted to increase her patience and her happiness, with my help she managed to achieve well*being* and a lot more. S was taking a number of medications and now, she doesn't take any! She is much more fun to be around, relaxed, and joyful. *She* is more satisfied with the way she relates to the world, the status of her relationships, her mood, and the positivity she attracts.

After seeing what S and I accomplished together in just a couple of years, I thought perhaps we could help other dogs and their humans increase their satisfaction with life and to have more fun together. I convinced S to help me write this book—she has thumbs, so writing goes a lot quicker with her help!

Whether you're coaching your human on their journey to well*being*, wishing to learn some mindfulness practices, or wanting to strengthen your bond, I hope you enjoy *How to Heal Your Human.*

Eamon the Wheaten
Conifer, Colorado
2019

INTRO

It probably goes without saying that S and I are a little "woo-woo." Nevertheless, we appreciate science and, in fact, she spends many of her days immersed in it! As previously mentioned, I believe all dogs have the capacity to be "therapy dogs." But you don't need to take my word for it—there is a lot of scientific evidence that supports this notion. For example:

- Pet ownership is associated with improved quality of life through social support, reduced depression, and other psychosocial predictors of health.[1]

- Pet owners have been found to report higher life satisfaction than non-owners.[2]

- Oxytocin is a neuropeptide found in mammals and is recognized for its role in bonding, socialization, and stress relief. Oxytocin causes many physiologic changes, including slowing heart rate and breathing, quieting blood pressure, inhibiting stress hormones, and creating a sense of calm, comfort, and focus. Studies have demonstrated that human–animal interaction increases oxytocin levels in the brain.[3,4,5]

This book is intended for dogs wishing to help their humans in their quest for well*being*. Please keep in mind, however, that there is no right or wrong way to use this book or even to achieve a peaceful, joyous existence. Likewise, if you're a human without a dog, that's perfectly fine. You can benefit from the text and you can do the mindfulness exercises on your own, with a stuffed dog, or possibly even with a cat.

Throughout the book, I use the term "universe." If you worship a god or have another term that resonates more for you than "universe," consider it interchangeable.

How to Heal Your Human is structured to mirror the journey I took with S, and it is a natural progression in mindfulness. Nevertheless, if your person is having difficulty with a particular concept, or if one concept is more relevant for their situation, feel free to move through the content in a non-linear fashion. Each chapter stands alone.

The chapter framework is designed to be easy to follow. Each chapter focuses on a concept that is key—in my humble opinion—to humans achieving satisfaction in their lives. There is a motivational quote at the beginning of each chapter, followed by text about my observations and experiences with humans, including but not limited to S. I've also included a mindfulness activity for you to try with your human. Each exercise is designed to help your human begin to see the relevance of the concept to their daily lives and the way they relate to the world. Finally, I offer two mantras, or affirmations, at the end of each chapter— one for you and one for your human. They are marked with the following icons:

If you and your human use traditional meditation techniques and you wish to repeat the mantra 108 times (or more) using a mala, that's great. For most of you, the affirmations will be there for you to use as reminders and reinforcements of the concepts I've presented as you work with them in your daily life. Feel free to appropriate them—or even discard them—as you work through the book.

Whether you're human or canine, not everything in this book will resonate for each of you, and that's okay. I hope you find something useful. I'd love nothing more than for your copy of *How to Heal Your Human* to sit "dog-eared" on your nightstand after years of use!

Finally, a word for you canine healers: please extend the same compassion to yourself that you do to your human. We all have different levels of tolerance for being touched, sitting quietly, and engaging in the various activities I suggest. Do what feels right for YOU. And now, go off and heel your human! I mean, *heal* your human!

1. Schreiner, PJ. Emerging Cardiovascular Risk Research: Impact of Pets on Cardiovascular Risk Prevention. Current Cardiovascular Risk Reports 10:8, 2016.

2. Bao, KJ, Schreer G. Pets and Happiness: Examining the Association between Pet Ownership and Wellbeing. Anthrozoös 29:283, 2016.

3. Miller, SC, et al. An examination of changes in oxytocin levels in men and women before and after interaction with a bonded dog. Anthrozoös 22:31, 2009.

4. Odendaal JS. Animal-assisted therapy—magic or medicine? Journal of Psychosomatic Research 49:275, 2000.

5. Odendaal, JS, Meintjes RA. Neurophysiological correlates of affiliative behaviour between humans and dogs. The Veterinary Journal 165:296, 2003.

AWARENESS

Awareness is the birthplace of possibility. Everything you want to do, everything you want to be, starts here.

—Deepak Chopra

I believe that for humans, what Deepak Chopra says is true. Humans are so funny sometimes. They go through life blissfully unaware. Have you ever observed one in heavy traffic at rush hour or seen one in the grocery store after work? They like to say they are "on a mission." When your human is "on a mission," so to speak, what that means is that they are singularly focused. And while that orientation serves humans well in certain situations, it usually results in their being unaware of much of what is going on around them. They are self-absorbed, thinking only about achieving their goal, whether it's getting to work on time (even though they departed late) or getting all the stuff on the grocery list and making it through the checkout line in record time. They don't see other people, other humans—not really—they see them as obstacles in their way.

As a result, humans don't notice. They don't observe. They miss out on lots of really cool things going on around them and overlook opportunities to enjoy the experience of living. It seems to me that part of the human experience is the shared experience with other beings, the recognition of the interconnectedness of all things. When humans get "busy," "stressed," or "overwhelmed," they move as if they are the only ones on earth—as if nothing else exists aside from them and their goal and whatever they need to achieve it. If your human is behaving this way—and they all do, from time to time—they may be "unconscious." I don't mean "unconscious" in the clinical sense. I mean unconscious in the spiritual sense. I mean unaware, unable to be present, short-tempered, deep in their own thoughts, unwilling or unable to acknowledge others … like that.

When we are aware, we have the ability to notice, observe, perceive. We are conscious. I submit that the quickest and most effective way for humans to achieve wellness—true well*being*—is to elevate their consciousness. Really, everything in this book is designed to help you help your human raise their consciousness. What does that mean? It means that if they use these tools, and possibly others they acquire elsewhere, they will learn to be present, to join the flow of creativity already going on around them. It means they will learn to take responsibility for their own well*being*, their own joy. They will exhibit and practice gratitude. They will be kinder and more compassionate. And then, they won't. And when they aren't, they will treat themselves with compassion and try again. And you, my fellow canine, can help them discover all the tools they already have to help them do that. Starting right now.

We're going to start our journey together with awareness, because as Deepak Chopra says, "it is the birthplace of possibility." It's where well*being* begins. The great news for us canine healers is that awareness is relatively easy—and fun—to teach a human. They may not be quick learners with all the concepts in this book, but most of them will get "awareness" fairly quickly. Here's a fun and rewarding exercise you can do with your human to begin to teach them how to notice and observe.

Sunrise

This is one of the simplest activities in this book. That said, it's very powerful. For my human, the most difficult part of this exercise was getting her out of bed in time to do it! Here's what you do: you watch the sunrise with your human. Yep—that's it! Here are a few guidelines for making the most of this activity:

- If you can do this exercise outside, please do so. It's not quite the same indoors, but it's better than not doing it at all.

- Please don't use music or headphones.

- Ask your human to leave their phone behind.

- It's okay if you aren't able to tolerate sitting quietly with your human for the duration of the activity, but please try to be as good a dog as possible so they can focus on what's happening around them, instead of shifting attention by either talking to or correcting you.

- It takes humans a bit of time to ease into an exercise like this, so I recommend getting them up at least 15 minutes before you're going to begin watching. Make sure they have whatever they need to be comfortable so their distractions are minimized. For example, a cushion or chair to sit on, a cup of coffee or tea … stuff like that.

- If you and your human can do this exercise as part of a hiking or camping trip in a beautiful spot, even better, you lucky dog!

As you're watching the sunrise together, coach your human to notice and observe. In this exercise, it's perfectly okay to name what they notice, but they should do so quietly, internally. Please limit talking. Help them to see, smell, taste, feel, and hear. For example, depending on where you do this exercise, they may hear birds chirping, children laughing, lawnmowers buzzing, or water rushing. They may taste pollen or dust. They may feel a cool breeze, the warmth of the sun, or even a mosquito bite. They may feel the temperature change as the sun rises and the light changes. They may see squirrels, ants, cars, and other people. They may notice different colors in the sky. They may smell a number of things such as smoke, bacon, rain, or fresh cut grass.

Sit and watch the sunrise as long as you can. Try to pick a day when your human doesn't have other commitments and they can just sit and be. You'll need a minimum of 15 minutes, but 30 minutes is better and an hour is ideal. When they are done, have them take three very deep breaths, filling up their belly and exhaling completely. Instruct them to pause for three seconds at the top and bottom of each breath. If they wish to acknowledge their gratitude for the day, the practice, and/or you, they should by all means do so. Ditto with prayer or meditation. If they wish to continue with deep breathing, that's great, too.

I am alert and present and ready to help my human. Do I hear a cheese wrapper?

I celebrate the interconnectedness of all things and my role in the universe.

SILENCE

Listen to silence. It has so much to say.

—Rumi

Did you know that many humans are in constant conversation? Like, seriously, nonstop. They incessantly chat-chat-chatter away, often inside their own heads. Sometimes, however, they are quite verbal with their chatter and, in fact, we dogs—and other pets, too—legitimize their chatter. We are such great listeners—amazing, really. Sometimes, they just can't help themselves—they talk to us all the time! I love the sound of S's voice. I love when she talks to me or sings to me. I love just being acknowledged. But I've also come to realize that when she can't turn off the chatter, she needs some extra help. It means her mind is on overload. It's running amok with thoughts.

Chattering isn't bad or wrong. But like many of the things we'll talk about in this book, it can prevent your human from being present. And when humans aren't present, they can't feel *anything*. They miss out on all the feels—joy and sadness, grief and enthusiasm. Just … nothing. Zilch. Nada. Zero.

Therefore, helping your human begin to experience silence is very useful in terms of their well*being*. Being well includes being able and willing to feel. For humans, it also includes making friends with their own minds. I'm not going to lie to you. As simple as this concept is, of all the things we'll explore together, it is the most challenging for many humans to learn. For example, S has been using various forms of meditation for over 20 years. She started as part of her Ashtanga yoga practice, dabbled in Zen Buddhism, and finally settled on a practice she learned from the renowned Buddhist teacher Pema Chödrön.

After all her years of study and practice, S remains very challenged by this technique and by silence in general. She recently did a 12-hour silence exercise, and to her surprise, she found it very difficult to stop talking—sometimes, even to inanimate objects. "I'm going to eat you now," she'd think to herself as she sat down to a bowl of stir-fried rice and veggies. "Hmm ... I wonder where I put that ribbon ... it must be here somewhere...." "Look! It's snowing again!" and, "Ugh. It's snowing *again*."

What's even more fascinating is that when she talks to me, she also answers! "What are you doing, E? Just hanging out? Oh, yes, you are the best hanger-outer in the world! Such a good boy you are, E! Let's go hang out in the other room. Oh, you want a treat? Of course you do. I can get you a treat!"

Constant, verbal and non-verbal chatter! Humans typically don't realize that silence is not just about talking. Silence is also about thinking. When your human can find even small glimpses of true silence—not only from sound, but also from thought—they will experience freedom, peace, and mindfulness.

We dogs are always present, in flow, living in the now. Because we don't have to prevent ourselves from thinking or talking, I have to rely a bit more on S for the human perspective on silence than I do for some of the other concepts in this book, so please keep that in mind as I relay her experience and my observations.

The type of meditation S learned from Pema Chödrön is called *shamatha-vipashyana* ("tranquility-insight"), and the way Ani Pema learned it was originally taught by Chögyam Trungpa Rinpoche. Whereas many meditation techniques use an object of focus that the practitioner comes back to repeatedly, this technique uses an *absence* of focus. It is very challenging for many Westerners like S, but even *attempting* it has great rewards.

S and I discussed simplifying these instructions even more for the purposes of this book, but S believes that they are about as simple as they are going to get. Because this is so challenging, we considered including a different exercise. To help us make a decision, we sent the draft chapter to two friends for review, both of whom are inexperienced with meditation. The chapter didn't resonate at all for one of them, but the other reported such a profound experience with the exercise we decided to include it and Ani Pema's instructions in their entirety.

It's important for your human to understand each element. This is a rigorous and traditional practice, so please encourage your person to modify as they see fit so it works for them. As an example, I've included some of S's modifications in the following section. See if your human will give it a try! It's a great practice for beginning to experience true silence.

Sitting in Silence

These instructions are from the book *When Things Fall Apart: Heart Advice for Difficult Times.*

Ani Pema discusses six points of posture and provides specific instructions for how to settle in by checking them. They include:

- Seat
- Legs
- Torso
- Hands
- Eyes
- Mouth

While they are in silence many humans struggle to stay active. That's one reason I included the full instructions. It's challenging for them to remain active but not be deep in their own thoughts. Likewise, some of them have a tendency to fall asleep when they finally relinquish their thoughts.

Here are instructions for the traditional technique:

1. Whether sitting on a cushion on the floor or in a chair, the seat should be flat, not tilting in any direction.

2. Legs are crossed comfortably in front of you—or if your person is sitting in a chair, their feet are flat on the floor, knees a few inches apart.

3. The torso, from the head to the seat, is upright with a strong back and an open front. If your person is sitting in a chair, it's best for them not to lean back. If they slouch, ask them to sit upright again or they can self-correct.

4. The hands are open, with palms down, resting on the thighs.

5. The eyes are open, in a soft gaze, slightly downward, approximately six feet in front.

6. The mouth is slightly open, the jaw is relaxed, and the top of the tongue is placed lightly on the roof of the mouth.

Tell your person to breathe normally, with attention lightly on the out-breath. As your human meditates quietly and silently, coach them to aim for an absence of thought. If their thoughts run on, tell them to take notice, then gently say "thinking" and let the thought go. They can return over and over again to the place where they have no thoughts.

I am extremely tolerant and will sit quietly with S while she meditates, literally for hours sometimes. I understand this is unusual, so please don't compare yourself to me. The key with this practice, as with any practice, is to help your human make it their own so it works for *them*. S has modified it a few ways over the years, as follows:

- S's body has changed a lot in 20 years. Now, when she sits cross-legged, she experiences a fair amount of hip pain. Because she really wants to continue to sit on the floor, S uses a Zafu, a special kind of cushion common amongst Zen practitioners. Any posture works, as long as your human can sit upright without pain.

- S prefers a mudra (hand position) that is less internally focused and more externally focused. Something more open. If your person is similar, they can try palms up or use any mudra they like. For that matter, they can just relax their hands as they wish.

- When S was beginning, she would aim for 20 minutes of meditation, which she says seemed like an eternity. Now, 20 minutes goes really quickly for her and she often declares it insufficient. Sometimes she sits for incredibly long periods of time. Your person should do what feels right to them. If they are new, suggest 10 minutes, which will likely seem much longer and is definitely enough time for them to experience benefits.

Encourage your person to use the practice of awareness we discussed in the previous chapter in conjunction with sitting in silence. By that, I mean it's often useful to reflect later on and become aware of what kept showing up in terms of thoughts. For S, what shows up tends to be lists … things to do, things to buy at the grocery store, meals for the week. I'll never understand the power of the "What's for dinner?" phenomenon, but humans really get hung up on that!

Also, it is absolutely critical that your person be gentle with themselves as they work with this practice. As outlined, it's a rigorous traditional meditation practice. Coach them to be kind and compassionate and not to berate themselves for thinking. I assure you, they will think. And sometimes, it will seem as if they spent their entire meditation period doing nothing but saying "thinking" to themselves over and over and over again. And that is perfectly fine.

 Hey! I only speak when I have something useful to say. Hey!

When my mind is still, I am peaceful and I am free.

COMPASSION

True compassion does not come from wanting to help out those less fortunate than ourselves, but from realizing our kinship with all beings.

—Pema Chödrön

Chances are if your person is open to your help and is reading this book with you, they are already practicing compassion—at least toward animals. I am frequently confounded by the fact that many people who show compassion toward animals often are unable or unwilling to demonstrate that same compassion toward other humans. I think it's because they believe that, unlike humans, we animals are less fortunate because we have so little control over our circumstances. Because humans have an unfortunate tendency to assign blame, they are very judgmental toward each other, and they mistakenly believe that their fellow humans "should know better" than to get themselves into the pickles they find themselves in.

And self-compassion? For humans, that's the hardest of all! They carry tremendous guilt and find it very difficult to forgive themselves, even for the simplest, most innocent transgressions. Many humans find it challenging to accept that they are worthy of peace, love, joy, and success—and forgiveness. This lack of self-compassion is nothing short of mind-boggling to me. Just think of all the things humans can do! They are walking, talking, singing, dancing miracles—with thumbs! They are amazing, if for no other reason than that they are human.

When we have self-compassion, we extend the same love, kindness, and understanding to ourselves that we do to others. This doesn't mean that we feel sorry for ourselves or wallow in our self-pity. Instead, it means that we are loving toward and accepting of ourselves—that we make friends with ourselves. We speak to ourselves with kindness.

For dogs, this is a rather foreign way of thinking because we are not conditioned the same way humans are. They are taught all kinds of silly things about how it is unbecoming to speak their own virtues and how they should not let their imperfections be seen. For your person, it is really, really important to learn the art of self-compassion—it is a critical part of healing and well*being*. According to Dr. Kristin Neff, PhD, an expert in self-compassion, self-compassion is associated with greater levels of happiness, optimism, life satisfaction, body appreciation, perceived competence, and motivation. Once your human learns self-compassion, they will discover that they have infinite amounts of love and care for others, including you. You'll be able to tell if your human is making progress in this area because they will stop over-apologizing and become more accepting of their humanity.

Learning self-compassion can be a long and arduous path for some humans. If that is the case for yours, it may go well beyond the scope of this book. Nevertheless, we can build on the compassion that readers of this book already have for animals to help them see how self-compassion opens the door for very deep, loving connections with all others, regardless of species.

Here is an exercise you and your human can work through together to strengthen your relationship through compassion. It will also help them begin to appreciate the miracle they are.

Doglen

Drawing from the Tibetan Buddhist practice of tonglen, "Doglen" is a lighthearted canine-friendly way of illustrating compassion for oneself and others. Tonglen essentially means *giving and taking*. In tonglen, the practitioner visualizes taking in the suffering of oneself and others upon inhaling their breath and giving compassion and love to all sentient beings as they exhale.

To do the Doglen exercise, have your human identify a place where they commonly feel some physical pain—physical pain is an easier place to start for most humans. For my people, this is usually the back, the head or the hips. Have them focus on that pain for a few moments.

Then, sit on the floor with your human. If they cannot sit on the floor, sit as close as you can get to them while they are sitting on a chair. They can use any posture that works for them.

Ask them to begin with three very deep breaths, filling up their belly and exhaling slowly and completely. If they wish to try practicing traditional tonglen, they can incorporate it at this stage. For example, they can breathe in the sickness of a friend or loved one, take that on, and then breathe out relaxation and healing. S often uses tonglen when she sees road kill—it makes her feel like she can do *something* about a rather sad situation and, perhaps, help the dead animal and others like it find peace. As your person builds their skill, they can take on more and more pain and suffering and exhale deeper compassion and loving kindness.

When they are ready to begin Doglen, sit or lie near them in a position that allows them access to the painful bit on you. For example, with S and her sore hips, I will lie near her and she will kneel near me. Then, encourage your person to mindfully work on that pain with you. In my case, S rubs my hips lovingly while maintaining deep breathing and visualizing her pain dissipating. When your human does this, they will notice that their compassion is easily transferable; that their compassion for animals is the very same compassion they can generate and offer to themselves and all others. In addition, your person may also find that their physical pain lessens with this exercise.

You may need to have self-compassion, too, as you work with Doglen. We all have different tolerance for this sort of exercise, so if you do not like to be massaged, scratched, or whatever, that's okay. Just have your person visualize this part of the exercise and they will benefit. When your person is complete with this portion of the exercise, have them sit quietly for a few moments before moving about. Encourage them to take a few moments to observe how their connection to others enhances their self-compassion and vice versa—it is a beautiful cycle!

A note on compassion and empathy:

When writing this book, I considered a chapter on empathy. After giving it a great deal of thought, I decided to include this chapter on compassion instead. This is because compassion goes beyond observation to include *action*. According to Thupten Jinpa, PhD, the Dalai Lama's principal English translator and author of the course Compassion Cultivation Training, compassion is a four-step process:

1. Awareness of suffering
2. Sympathetic concern related to being emotionally moved by suffering
3. Wish to see the relief of that suffering
4. Responsiveness or readiness to help relieve that suffering

I designed Doglen to be consistent with this process. Your human can use the process above any time they wish to cultivate compassion, and thus compassion can become a practice for them. The same principles apply when they wish to cultivate self-compassion—they will just need to be sympathetic to their own suffering.

 I have the best human ever! They take me out every day so I can read my pee-mail!

 I am the miracle my dog believes me to be.

Courage

Every time we choose courage, we make everyone around us a little better and the world a little braver.

—Brené Brown

When we are courageous, we feel fear, but we forge ahead anyway. We exhibit bravery and strength, despite experiencing pain or grief. Courage is a very powerful quality, and it is one of the few that I believe humans and canines experience similarly.

We canines are always present, that's for sure. And like humans, we also feel fear. Thunderstorms? Fireworks? Gunshots? Yep, those can evoke feelings of distress. However, with some coaxing and love, we can usually move through it. *(Okay, maybe not with fireworks.)*

Your risk-averse human is much the same. Their fear and attachment to the predictable gets in the way of their ability— and willingness—to experience love, joy, and peace. Instead, they grasp, force, and try to produce all kinds of situations— even ones that ultimately bring them dissatisfaction.

Did I mention humans crave stability? They believe that we dogs are creatures of habit—and while it is true that we usually thrive in routine, humans set a new standard in choosing comfort over the unknown. Most of them don't really like surprises. They want to "get into a groove," so they have to experience as little change as possible. *(I submit that there's a fine line between a groove and a rut, but …)* Humans always want to know what to anticipate so they can plan ahead, thereby exerting as much control as is feasible.

What humans often don't understand or consider is that change is inevitable because everything is impermanent. And I mean *everything.* Ever hear a human say "All things happen for a reason?" They say that in times of trouble so they feel better about not getting what they want or thought they wanted. Rarely does one utter, "All things happen for a reason" when they are living their dream. But it's the same. "This, too, shall pass" applies to *all life, all situations, and all relationships.*

In her book *Living Beautifully with Uncertainty and Change,* Pema Chödrön, the beloved Buddhist teacher, states:

> But it's not impermanence per se, or even knowing we're going to die, that is the cause of our suffering, the Buddha taught. Rather, it's our *resistance to the fundamental uncertainty of our situation.* Our discomfort arises from all of our efforts to put ground under our feet, to realize our dream of constant okayness. When we resist change, it's called suffering. But when we can completely let go and not struggle against it, when we can embrace the groundlessness of our situation and relax into its dynamic quality, that's called *enlightenment,* or awakening to our true nature, to our fundamental goodness. Another word for this is *freedom*—freedom from struggling against the fundamental ambiguity of being human.

Embracing change, achieving freedom, and celebrating impermanence are all acts of courage. All of these result in our humans being happier and more loving. When they can begin to do these things, they will see that the world around them is beautiful not in spite of its impermanence, but *because* of it. Case in point? Bubbles.

Bubbles

Bubbles. They are beautiful and unique—and like snowflakes, no two are the same. They are just incredible the way they reflect light, color, and images. They are weightless and stunning. Some last longer than others, but they have a shockingly short existence. And guess what? We love them anyway! Kids love them, adults love them, and dogs love them. Heck, I wouldn't know, but I'll bet even cats love bubbles.

So herein lies one of the simplest and the most challenging activities you'll find in this book. *Get your human to blow some bubbles with you.* That's it. Make some, buy some—it doesn't really matter where you acquire them. Just blow some bubbles.

And now, for the tricky part: as you and your human blow bubbles together, take care to notice the unique qualities of each bubble. Observe how beautiful they are, how they float this way or that, how the wind blows them. Notice how they appear as different colors—blue, pink, purple. Celebrate each and every bubble, whether it just pops in midair, or it hits an object and meets the end of its existence. Maybe you try to catch it, or bite at it, and the bubble is no more. Ask your human to let each one go, despite its awesomeness.

Then, take a minute to reflect on this experience.

See? That wasn't so hard, was it? It was probably enormous fun! Encourage your human to close their eyes, take a few deep breaths, and make a mental note of how this moment feels. Next time they are faced with unwanted impermanence, see if they can replicate this feeling of okayness. Invite them to acknowledge and celebrate the impermanence and even the loss of something they wanted, or found beautiful. It's the impermanence that makes something beautiful to us.

Bubbles are awesome because they are inexpensive and accessible to all of us. You can do this exercise on an as-needed basis, you can make it a practice, and/or your human can even use bubbles as a visualization technique when they are somewhere inappropriate for blowing bubbles.

The better our humans get at embracing the inherent impermanence of beauty, the more courageous they become. The more courageous our humans become and the more willing they are to love, celebrate, and appreciate in the full knowing that moments, situations, and relationships *won't* last, the more spontaneous joy they will feel and the happier they will be.

Courage is not domain-specific. Once your human is skilled at cultivating courage, they'll be braver in love, in their friendships, and in their work. And, as Brené says, the world will be a little braver.

I'm a good dog, even though I ate that Italian sandal. I was just helping my human understand impermanence.

I am brave, daring, and calm.

SURRENDER

If you surrendered to the air, you could ride it.

—Toni Morrison

One of the most fascinating things about humans is how much control they think they have. They spend so much time forcing outcomes and trying to "make things happen," despite uncontrollable circumstances.

I maintain the illusion of control is the source of much dissatisfaction and unhappiness for them. Humans wonder why situations and events do not go their way or live up to their expectations, especially if they have put forth a lot of effort in attempting to gain control. They often have a plan, a carefully developed scheme for how they are going to accomplish some goal. By investing so much in devising The Plan, they are reluctant or even unable to abandon it, even when it is unattainable or when a different path would produce even greater satisfaction.

When things do not go according to The Plan, they have quite a bit of difficulty surrendering to what *is* and recognizing the beauty in every moment of now. Their perspective is obscured by their vision and their intense attachment to it.

In contrast, we canines already realize that we control very little—we have to rely on our humans to feed us, bathe us, and keep us safe and healthy. It's just the way it is in our world, and guess what? Most of the time we are naturally happy. We are joyful. It is not in spite of our lack of control. *It's because of it.*

Surrender is not something that humans usually learn easily. This is mostly because they have a weird recursive relationship with the notion of giving up control. What I mean by that is they think if they surrender "correctly" or "do it right," things will "turn around" and they will get what they want. What they don't realize is that most of the time, they are getting what they want and need but they are so busy trying to execute The Plan, they don't even see it.

When they finally *do* see it and allow things to happen, they will experience something called *flow*. We dogs don't really use this notion because we are in flow nearly all the time.

You will know when your person is in flow because they will be happy, positive, energized, and engaged in whatever they are doing at the moment. They will be fully present and able to enjoy just being and doing, without worrying about things being perfect according to The Plan. They will smile more and complain a lot less.

Good thing we canines are naturally patient, because this may take a little time. Please be patient with your human because they often have very long, storied histories with control. I have never met a single one who did not have to work to relinquish control!

Here is a mindfulness exercise you can try with your human to help them relinquish control and begin to see the beauty and joy of flow. S loves this exercise because she can include all the dogs she has ever loved, not just me. This exercise is designed to help your person surrender to guidance and help from the universe.

The Crystal Dog Bowl

Start by sitting on the floor with your human, or if they cannot sit on the floor, sit as close as you can get to them while they are sitting on a chair. Any posture that works for them can be used. They just need to be comfortable.

To begin, they will pet you very softly for whatever amount of time feels appropriate to them and that you can tolerate—ideally a minute or two. Then, have them close their eyes and begin with three very deep breaths, filling up their belly and exhaling slowly and completely. Ask them to hold their breath for three full seconds at the top and bottom of each breath.

When they are ready, have them visualize you, your predecessor(s), or a pack of all the dogs they have ever loved as angels. Make this fun! They can envision the canine angels as funny, serious, lifelike, cartoons—whatever brings them comfort. Have them sit with this vision for a moment and just take it in. Ask them to remember all the love and care they gave to their dog(s) and prepare to allow the canines to reciprocate.

Have them imagine the canine angels sitting in front of a crystal dog bowl. They may even be wagging. As its name suggests, the crystal dog bowl is full of prismatic light, shimmering and inviting. Have them just take that in for a moment. Then, help your human put whatever is troubling them or whatever they would like help with into the crystal dog bowl. For example, when S was looking for a job, she put her whole career—all the accomplishments, relationships, titles, expertise, and knowledge, including her computer bag—into the crystal dog bowl. Assure your human the crystal dog bowl is magical and there is nothing too big to go in it. It expands naturally!

Once your human has put their issue/situation/desire/ relationship into the crystal dog bowl, have them envision the canine angels picking it up and flying away with it.

This exercise can also involve more than one human. S and P have used The Crystal Dog Bowl together when they had high expectations for a specific day. They let their previous dog, Gimli, design the day for them and they agreed to accept his goofball-style help. It worked miraculously! They renounced their expectations, gave up The Plan, and felt Gim's presence. They had such fun envisioning him in control of the day.

Humans usually feel an immediate sense of relief at no longer believing they are or have to be the one in control. They can focus on other stuff such as choosing joy, or being in flow—things that they actually *can* control. They can then visualize themselves in a state of peace and love with the point of consternation no longer their concern. If they wish, they can verbalize that they are grateful to the dog(s) and the universe for being willing to take their issue on for them. Recommend that your human also verbalize that they are willing to accept the help and that they will stop trying to control timing and outcomes—even if the help arrives differently that they envisioned. Finally, they should end the meditation with three deep breaths and some pets, just as they started.

The Crystal Dog Bowl is a powerful exercise because by using it, the human is sending a very clear message to the universe that they are ready to relinquish control of said situation and let the universe and the dogs (we're conduits to the universe, as you know) handle it. However—and this is very important— you must coach your human that once they have relinquished control to the universe, they cannot attempt to take it back. That sends a very clear message to the universe that they are not, in fact, willing to relinquish control and that they are not ready for guidance. It is a distrustful move.

It may take a few tries for your person to get the hang of this, so please be patient. Most importantly, please coach your human to be patient with themselves as they embark on a new way of being. Impatience and control are inconsistent with surrender and flow. Just like darkness and light, they cannot coexist.

 I trust the universe. After all, the universe created dogs.

 I don't need The Plan because the universe is in charge and I trust the universe.

FLOW

Don't worry that it's not good enough for anyone else to hear. Just sing. Sing a song.

—Joe Raposo, *Sing* (written for Sesame Street, popularized by The Carpenters)

It may come as a surprise to you, but many humans do not regularly experience flow. In fact, many humans don't even know flow is a thing. They just know that sometimes they don't have to try so hard to be present. For us dogs, that is crazy! Just nuts! We *live* in flow. We are constantly present, free from worry, planning, strategy, outcomes … we just *are*, being and doing. Ever see one of us riding in the car with our head out the window? Yeah, that's flow. We are not thinking about what is for dinner. *(Chances are because we already know, but that's beside the point.)*

Positive psychologist Mihaly Csikszentmihalyi describes flow as "a state of complete immersion in an activity." He says that in flow, the mental state is such that we are "completely involved in an activity for its own sake. The ego falls away. Time flies. Every action, movement, and thought follows inevitably from the previous one, like playing jazz. Your whole being is involved and you are using your skills to the utmost."[6]

My peeps love jazz! They have historically experienced flow while listening to improvised music, such as jazz and jam bands. They are also frequently in a state of flow when they are fly fishing, skiing, snowboarding, hiking, or cooking. And cycling— especially mountain biking. But your person need not do any of these things to experience flow.

The thing is, *any* activity can be conducted in mindfulness, and flow can be experienced while doing anything. From showering, to mowing the lawn, to doing laundry, anything at all can induce flow. We dogs are always in flow, whether we're sleeping, dreaming, eating, or playing! We epitomize mindfulness.

Since so many humans have difficulty letting go and finding flow, you may need to nudge your person along a bit. They may not find it on their own, but you can encourage them to cultivate flow. Once they experience it in a cultivated setting, they will recognize it more easily when it "just happens." Here is a really fun activity you can do with your person to help them notice, observe, and experience flow.

6. Geirland J. Go With The Flow. Wired 4.09, 1996.

Just Sing

Start by having your person cue some music that includes lyrics they know well. This could be an album or a Spotify playlist or even a radio station. S likes to use a Pandora station with a lot of 70s music, like the Bee Gees, Michael McDonald, Ambrosia, The Carpenters. Stuff like that. Have the music ready to go, but do not turn it on just yet. Start by sitting on the floor with your human, or if they cannot sit on the floor, sit as close as you can get to them while they are sitting on a chair. They can use any posture that works for them. Standing is even fine for this because they should not get too comfortable.

To begin, they should pet you and muss up your fur, maybe begin with a scratch behind the ears. They should do this for whatever amount of time feels appropriate to them and that you can tolerate—ideally a minute or two. Then, ask them to begin with three very deep breaths, filling up their belly and exhaling slowly and completely. Ask them to hold their breath for three full seconds at the top and bottom of each breath. The goal with these breaths is simply to relax and let go of any expectations whatsoever—especially expectations of getting this "right."

The goofier your human is, the more fun both of you will have and the quicker you'll find flow, punctuated with lots of laughter. Like most dogs, I *love* the sound of my person's voice. S has a great memory and consequently, she knows the words to many, many songs across genres and eras. She loves almost all music. Sadly, she is a terrible singer. But like most of her friends, I love when she sings anyway, because that means she is *really* relaxed!

When they are ready, have your human turn the music on and stand up or at least get into a position where they can move. This is where things get really fun! Ask them to sing to you. But not the words to the songs as they know them. Instead, ask them to modify the lyrics just for you. If you are a small dog, they can even pick you up and dance with you while they are singing to you. S sort of dances around me while she is singing to me. This should all be done spontaneously because that is where your person will find flow.

Here are a couple of examples from my recent experience with S. As I mentioned, like a lot of children of the 70s, she knows the words to every Bee Gees song. She recently sang *More than a Wheaten* to me, to the tune of *More than a Woman*. When doing this, she does not get hung up on stuff, and she does not practice in advance—that would defeat the purpose. Part of what makes a Pandora station work so well for this is that she doesn't know what song is coming next!

Another example is *Everybody's Working for the Wheaten* to Loverboy's *Everybody's Working for the Weekend* and *Lovely Dog* to the tune of Bill Wither's *Lovely Day*. *(Or, as close to the tunes as she could get, poor thing.)* I love the sound of her voice and the fact that she is paying attention just to me. Plus, she finds flow. This activity can be done anywhere there is music, including in the car. Love songs seem to work particularly well, but your human should use whatever music from whatever genre moves them. You both will know when it is time to complete this activity, but try for a minimum of three songs.

I live in every moment of now. Look! Here comes another one!

My energy is positive, my mind is at ease, and I am in the flow of creativity.

Joy

Joy is a decision, a really brave one, about how you are going to respond to life.

—Wess Stafford

S and I have a friend who recently told us that she has decided to focus on creating stability in her life because joy seemed too lofty a goal. *Oh, dear.* S and I believe our friend has this upside down. This may completely blow your human's mind, but here goes: joy is a *choice* they make. One of the few things they have control over is how they approach the world. And the world is naturally unstable. It's dynamic. Let that sink in for a minute. That's right—it's not something that they earn or don't or that's given to them or isn't. They choose joy. Or not.

Sometimes humans may be in such a state of flow that they don't have to choose—they're just joyful. That's awesome, but other times it won't work that way and they'll need to make a conscious decision about how they are going to move. Are they going to move forward in anger and resentment, or in love and joy? Of course, like many of the concepts we've discussed on our journey together, this one is recursive, too. The more often they choose joy, the more often they'll find themselves simply being joyful.

I believe that many humans are so fearful that they don't *allow* themselves to choose joy. They don't give themselves permission, and no one else is going to give them permission to choose joy, either. If they choose joy and it doesn't "stick," then they will find themselves disappointed, unhappy, perhaps even heartbroken and grieving.

First, the bad news: it won't stick. Joy, like everything, is impermanent. Advise your human to choose it anyway. Now, the good news: when they are able to relinquish fear and choose joy, they are likely to become someone they can live with—someone worthy of their own compassion. In choosing joy, they will approach the world with an open heart, open eyes, and open mind. They will experience more creativity and abundance than they ever thought possible. They will be someone they want to be. Someone other people want to be around. Someone other people want to work with. Someone other people want to be friends with. And then, they won't, because it won't stick. But that's okay, because once they know how to choose joy, they will get better and better at doing so and life for them will just get easier.

In her book *The Universe Has Your Back*, Gabrielle Bernstein talks about choosing joy, over and over again. This is a really powerful notion because humans can choose joy *any time* they wish, in *every moment* of now. Gabby says, "In any moment, no matter how far down the negative path of fear you've gone, you can choose again. You can always choose again." S and I hold tremendous gratitude for Gabby and her thinking, which was the impetus for the visualization below.

The Slot Machine O'Joy

The Slot Machine O'Joy is the best game ever! You never put any money in and you can spin again and again and again. Results may vary upon the initial spin, but ultimately, it is played until all the reels yield joy. Only good stuff comes out and not only is your human always a winner, but the universe wins, too! The world wins. Their friends and family win. You win. The Slot Machine O'Joy offers huge payouts with amazing odds.

I developed this technique for S when she was working with joy and learning to choose. Below, I've provided instructions for the first time you do it. Once your human has this visual ready to hand, they can use it whenever they wish, whether you're present or not. There are days when S uses it many times and some days, some really awesome ones, where she doesn't use it at all.

The first time you do this with your person, start by sitting on the floor with them, or if they cannot sit on the floor, sit as close as you can get to them while they are sitting on a chair. Any posture that works for them can be used. They just need to be comfortable.

To begin, they will pet you very softly for whatever amount of time feels appropriate to them and that you can tolerate—ideally a minute or two. Then, have them close their eyes and begin with three very deep breaths, filling up their belly and exhaling slowly and completely. Ask them to hold their breath for three full seconds at the top and bottom of each breath.

Next, coach them to visualize you sitting at a slot machine—S likes the old-school kind, with handles. She envisions three reels with no payline—she's always the winner, after all! Pull the handle for your person and tell them to watch the reels spin and imagine the sounds they make.

This is important: spin until you get the results your human needs. Sometimes, if it is a tough day for S, and she asks me to spin, we might get one anger, one resentment, and one guilt. But I spin. And I pull that handle for her over and over again until we get three joys. When we reach three joys, everyone wins!

I choose joy in every moment, but it's easiest when my human walks in the door.

I have the courage to choose joy.

GRATITUDE

Gratitude is the healthiest of all human emotions. The more you express gratitude for what you have, the more likely you will have even more to express gratitude for.

—Zig Ziglar

This is a book about healing and wellness, so Zig Ziglar's thinking really resonates with me. To be fair, S has had a daily gratitude practice for over 20 years. I've learned as much from her as she's learned from me, on this one.

Part of what makes gratitude so "healthy," as Zig puts it, is that in gratitude, we are thankful simply for what is—all the big and little things we have in our lives that make it rich. We appreciate others and we show kindness and compassion for each other. In gratitude, we truly want to contribute to others and to share our good fortune. And we all have good fortune. This philosophy, this way of being, is healthy for us as dogs and humans and healthy for our world. When we are grateful, we take great care with ourselves, with others, and with our planet. We are good friends, good coworkers, good family members, and good community members when we are thankful.

According to an article published by Harvard Medical School, "Gratitude is a thankful appreciation for what an individual receives, whether tangible or intangible. With gratitude, people acknowledge the goodness in their lives. In the process, people usually recognize that the source of that goodness lies at least partially outside themselves. As a result, gratitude also helps people connect to something larger than themselves as individuals—whether to other people, nature, or a higher power."[7]

The term "attitude of gratitude" doesn't really work for me because I believe that gratitude is not an attitude. Gratitude is a *practice*; it's a *commitment*. That doesn't mean that your person needs to *always* be in gratitude. That said, the more gratitude they practice, the more gratitude they'll have and the more great stuff is likely to happen for them.

As we close our journey together, I wish to acknowledge the impressive and talented folks who helped me bring this book to fruition. You can learn more about all of us in the section I called *Meet the Team*. I also wish to express my gratitude for all of you reading this book for your trust and openness. And of course, I want to thank the universe for bringing me to S and for all that we've accomplished together in the last three years since I came to live with her and P. It was a gift to be able to help S relinquish fear and resentment so we now live a life that is mostly full of joy and success and love. We have amazing friends. We appreciate our beautiful, peaceful home with a close connection to nature where we live with our beloved P.

Throughout this book, I've offered very specific, prescriptive instructions on mindfulness activities for you to try with your person. If you've made it this far, you're no doubt ready to begin designing your own practices, so I'll close with a few ideas for your consideration, which I hope you'll find helpful. I hope these ideas will be the foundation from which you and your human create your very own practices.

Gratitude Practice

Having a gratitude practice is one of the simplest and easiest ways to relinquish negativity and cultivate positive energy. S starts and ends most days with practices she's had for a long time. The tricky thing for her is to refrain from being compulsive about the practice or to try to "get it right." I have to work with her a bit to encourage her not to treat herself unkindly if she misses a day or falls asleep before she completes the practice. Please do the same for your person. After some time, they will likely notice that things just go better for them when they are in gratitude and they will want to do their practice. If they forget or don't feel like doing it some days, that's okay. Please be patient with them.

Gratitude Journal

Keeping a gratitude journal is a fun way not only to log the things your person is grateful for, but also to include the things they imagine you are grateful for. It provides historical background, and for some people, it is really interesting to look back and see what they were thinking at a different point in time. Some people make up all sorts of rules, such as that you name a certain number of things per day or that you can't name the same thing twice. Get creative! You can do this in groups, too, with friends or even with other dogs and their humans, which would be very courageous, indeed.

Gratitude Notes

Encourage your person to send notes of gratitude on a regular basis. Not just when someone does something extraordinary for them or buys them a fabulous gift—just whenever they feel appreciation for who someone *is* to them. This is a great way to spread gratitude, and it builds great relationships.

Gratitude Jar, Scrapbook, Board, Locket

To make a gratitude jar or box, all you need to do is find a jar or box, decorate it however you like, and keep a pen and some paper near it. Vases are fun for this because they are a reminder of the original gift of flowers—they keep the gift going long after the impermanent flowers have gone. Whenever your person thinks of something they are grateful for, they write it on the paper and put the paper in the vessel. Then, on a day when they maybe aren't feeling so hot or need a little extra encouragement, they can pick some or all of the papers out and read them. They can even take it a step further and use the papers, along with photos or images cut from a magazine, to make a gratitude board or scrapbook. S has a necklace she uses the same way—it's a spherical silver locket and she will write notes of gratitude or mantras or affirmations on little notes of paper, put them in the locket, and wear it when she wants to keep something top of mind.

Volunteer

When we volunteer, whether on a one-time project or on an ongoing basis, we are giving thanks for something we hold dear. I am so grateful to Jefferson County Open Space (JCOS) for allowing me the opportunity to be a Bark Patroller and to volunteer with S to preserve and protect our trails and to be ambassadors for responsible dog ownership. Maybe you, too, can find work that soothes your soul and fosters something you believe in. If you're as lucky as I am, you'll strengthen your bond with your human along the way!

7. Harvard Health Publishing. Giving thanks can make you happier. www.health.harvard.edu/healthbeat/giving-thanks-can-make-you-happier. Accessed June 22, 2019.

I am grateful for my human, and I'm going to put my slimy toy in her lap to show my appreciation.

 I am thankful for my canine companion, and I am grateful to the universe for watching over me, for guiding me, and for showing me the way.

EPILOGUE

Toward the end of the content development phase of this book, S had what she calls a "shitty" or a "tough" week. It wasn't that anything *bad* happened. In fact, a lot of *great* stuff happened that week. Even so, she was irritable, short-tempered, and impatient. When S says she has a "tough" time with something, what that usually means is that *she* is not satisfied with the way she is dealing with the constellation of events, activities, and relationships in her life. She understands that nothing is naturally "bad" or inherently stressful—it's how she deals with something (or doesn't) that makes it "tough." During this period, she used her practices—all of them, including a few not mentioned in this book—but she remained unsettled and grouchy. As the week ended, she found herself interrupting her meditation to kill an ant that had crawled on her! This may not seem like a big deal, but S does not believe it was okay to do that.

My observation is that when humans are in the state S was in during her "tough" week, they are *struggling with their own humanity.* I understand this deeply because I struggle with my dogdom—I'm writing a book, after all! But we are who we are in this life, and I believe it's best to surrender to our lot and find joy wherever we can. S knows *intellectually* that she is human, but that doesn't stop her from putting enormous pressure on herself from time to time and sometimes trying to be a superhero, though she rarely recognizes it in the moment and doesn't articulate it that way, ever. She works very hard to relinquish her perfection complex but it creeps in occasionally.

I suspect your human is much the same because, well, your human is *human*. They will sometimes have tough times, shitty weeks, and they will be deeply disappointed in how they react to things. And they may—like S—hold tremendous guilt for having ended the life of another sentient being in anger and frustration. Yes. *Even* an ant. What you and your human must understand is that this book is intended to help you on a quest for peace and well*being*; I've provided some thinking and tools for you to use to promote healing. Your human's well*being* may require more effort than reading a book written by a dog. Also, being "healed" does not mean that your person is no longer human. No matter how much they practice, they will continue to struggle with their own humanity sometimes because that's part of the human experience. Hopefully, though, with some new thinking and practices, they'll suffer a bit less and enjoy life a lot more.

If you wish to continue to help your human on their path to well*being*, I've included some of our favorite resources in the section that follows. Not surprisingly, I've called it *Resources*.

RESOURCES

Brené Brown
Dare to Lead: Brave Work. Tough Conversations. Whole Hearts.
The Gifts of Imperfection: Let Go of Who You Think You're Supposed to Be and Embrace Who You Are

Pema Chödrön
When Things Fall Apart: Heart Advice for Difficult Times
Living Beautifully: with Uncertainty and Change

Dr. Kristin Neff
self-compassion.org

Drs. Kristin Neff and Christopher Germer
The Mindful Self-Compassion Workbook: A Proven Way to Accept Yourself, Build Inner Strength, and Thrive

Compassion Cultivation Training
The Center for Compassion and Altruism Research and Education (Stanford University)
ccare.stanford.edu/education/about-compassion-cultivation-training-cct/

The Compassion Institute
www.compassioninstitute.com/the-program/compassion-cultivation-training/

Gabrielle Bernstein
The Universe Has Your Back: Transform Fear to Faith

David Hawkins

Letting Go: The Pathway of Surrender

Deena Kastor

Let Your Mind Run: A Memoir of Thinking My Way to Victory

The Human Animal Bond Research Institute (HABRI)

habri.org

Coach Kim Eickhoff

A great friend and ongoing resource for me and S, Kim developed and teaches a proprietary methodology called SHiFT that helps people relinquish fear and achieve freedom in their work and their lives.

Email: KimEickhoff@actioncoach.com

Roger Haston

Roger is a dear friend and provided invaluable consult on the content included in this book. He is a nationally recognized thought leader and speaker on animal welfare and currently serves as the President of The Institute for Animals.

Email: RHaston@TheInstituteForAnimals.org

Meet the Team

Eamon the Wheaten

Eamon the Wheaten is a Colorado-based canine author and trail advocate and is a volunteer ambassador for JCOS. As a Bark Patroller, he works to raise awareness of the impact of dogs on trails, model responsible dog behavior, and educate park visitors on bite prevention and dog safety. In 2018, he was nominated for the prestigious Gamble Oak Pioneer Award, which honors pioneering efforts to preserve and protect open-space lands.

Sandra Marticio

Sandra holds an interdisciplinary BA from the College of Arts and Letters at Michigan State University, where she studied English, Philosophy, and Communication and earned a Women's Studies Thematic. Her background includes scientific and clinical education, and she works as a business developer and healthcare communications strategist. She also designs and crafts artful bespoke malas and spiritual jewelry.

Churmy Fan

Churmy's illustrations are beloved by the Wheaten community, where she actively participates in conversations to raise awareness of the breed, including training, nutrition, and common health issues. She is a PhD candidate in Neuroscience at the University of Calgary and holds an MSc in Cell and Developmental Biology and a BSc in Animal Biology from the University of British Columbia. Churmy lives in Calgary with her husband and two Soft-Coated Wheaten Terriers, who compete in agility, rally obedience, and conformation. She is also an aspiring groomer. *(Basically, Churmy is good at everything except bowling.)*

Kate Agathon

Kate holds a PhD in Curriculum and Instruction from Purdue University, where she also obtained an MSEd in Curriculum and Instruction. She studied History at Colorado State University, where she got her BA. Kate works as a freelance writer in the outdoor recreation industry and is passionate about bicycling, conservation, diversity issues, animal welfare, and social justice. She can often be found in Colorado's wilderness with her rescue Blue "Healer" and PhDog, Utah.

Shaun Howard

Shaun is the Ranger Lead at Jefferson County Open Space, where she is responsible for training, leading, and mentoring the 300 volunteer Park Patrollers who support Open Space staff in ensuring the safety and enjoyment of the 7 million people who visit the 28 parks in the JCOS system each year. Shaun founded the Bark Patroller program, a landmark initiative of specially screened and trained dogs and their handlers who work as ambassadors throughout the parks and at special events. Shaun is very active in animal welfare and adoption. She teaches both human and canine first aid and CPR. Shaun enjoys long walks and relaxing on her rooftop deck with her two rescue pups, Avery and Baxter, who have rescued her many times in her life.

Greg Feldman

Greg's multi-faceted background was invaluable on this project, where he provided editing, publication consult, and photography services. Greg has an MA in Journalism and Mass Communication from The University of Colorado at Boulder and a BA in English from Binghamton University. His publishing background includes work for McGraw-Hill, and he has an extensive background as a medical editor. Greg is the owner of Phylum Photography, where he specializes in capturing the essence and personalities of well-loved pets. He lives in Colorado with his wife, two daughters, and a menagerie of rescue animals including dogs, cats, fish, snakes, lizards, pigs, birds, frogs, and at least one tortoise.

Patrick Scheff

Patrick played an integral role in this project from the moment of inception and was responsible for content development strategy, layout, publication, and marketing. He holds a degree in Advertising from Michigan State University, where he graduated with honors, and a Certificate in Communication Technology from the Colorado Institute of Arts. Patrick is a document production expert, specializing in informational graphics and data depiction for scientific and medical communications. He lives with Eamon and Sandra in Colorado, where he is an avid skier, mountain biker, and hockey player.

Made in the USA
Middletown, DE
25 January 2022